Orbs

A Collection of Poetry

Frederick E. Whitehead

No Frills

<<<>>>

Buffalo

Nofrillsbuffalo.com

Printed in the United States of America

Whitehead, Frederick E.
Orbs/ Whitehead- 2nd Edition

ISBN 978-0615594262

No Frills Buffalo Press
119 Dorchester Buffalo, New York
14213

Visit Nofrillsbuffalo.com

Cover art © 2011 David Thiel

For Tammy

old angels

old angels
emptying pans
of collected tears
out of windows
this is the rain I
look up through
if I squint hard enough
I can just make out
their silhouettes in
candle lit towers
shaking out the last drops
wiping the hair from their
eyes and closing the shutters

If I found myself
horrendously alone

would you be the stone in my shoe?
right between the little toe
and ring toe
would you then
make it a point to
clarify that there
is no such thing
as a ring toe
if I truly was that alone
would you be
the cheese on my fries
or the wood in my shed
would you care enough
to have the coroners
number on speed dial
just in case I really
screwed up?
if I found myself to be
that enormously alone
would you be the
bloodshot in my eyes
my warm morning beer
my cool evening shade
the ache for my head
or possibly an arcade for
for my pennies?
I'm just asking this because
if I ended up so gargantuanly alone
I think I might need
someone for my knit cap
the kind with the
ear flap things and
ridiculously long tassel
or at the very least,
if I was so universally alone,

someone
to bump into me
in the dark hallway of
middle night
so I could have the
chance to say
hey, get out of here

No. 5

Joe said,
pointing,
Creeley lived
there
brick, read word built
deep eye black
chemical
no. 5

easy boy

the window,
a timpani
under the mallets of
nor' east winds
pinned I lay, 'neath
63 pounds of
variegated blanketry
'tween the door
and bed, the dog

runs in his sleep
he is free in some
nocturnal field
the light from
the hallway catches a glint
of fang as he warns off
some unseen foe
as I lay nearly
immobile he is double clutching
into a higher gear
spinning nearly 360
degrees on the rag
rug by the door

another burst sends
his snout into the doorframe
he jumps up and looks
around for his enemy
thunder mates with
rattling glass, and
as the crescendo rises
he turns toward me,
still not quite awake

in this most gothic
of nights,
I fear
that
is not a smile
he is showing me

listen

where the valley road dipped
below rhododendron
voice
sweet as
gospel from the dale there came,
I stand in vest and crisp
collar, what hue would
describe this light
that drifted along
the ridgeline I
followed, to
stand here now
listening

Isadora

the peach balloon
with wide white ribbon
settled, when the breeze
died, near the
sewer grate at the edge
of my drive
in one of those mysterious
moments, my mind
rifled through all of
the index cards in its
inventory,
a name surfaced
in a whisper

Isadora

had it not been for an
unfortunate convergence of
design, you would
not have been transformed into
morbid fascinations
of odd death
what, if anything did you
see of the moment, before
your most attended to
attribute came to rest
near a curb in Nice

my guess is that
the modern choreography
of social order and vanity
mattered naught
as your eyes stared

unblinking at the
shocked citizenry

so, even now,
because of silk and circumstance,
we remember
less of the contents of the head
than we do the contents of the scarf

when unsure

the recognition
of love,
it lets itself be
known
a spark traveling
the surface of an eye
cobalt dove
taking rise
on thermals
of whispered words

Bullet

I will,
on my soulless
trek through sinew
flesh muscle bone,
leave a burning wake
of exponential sorrow
breath
a breath docile
now
for I am done,
be delivered
as I have before
put no blame to me,
I am the message
not the message maker
I was not sent for,
in or by way of peace
regardless of
mindless mantra
I am
but the
latest form of
capsulated ideology,
traveling 2346 feet per second
I am
the
common
denominator

the great migration

there may be no
accurate way to
measure the thrill
and relief that fills
the heart of the springbok
as she clears the croc
at waters edge
or the image that
was forming for her
of the grand promise of
the great migration,
as she leapt in a
a flight so graceful
a face full of springboky smile
toward a clear sky
fields of tall grass and
bright flowers unfurled
ahead of her,
stretching to horizon,
clear streams and refreshing breezes
shade of trees and mating waited
all of this
could only be matched, possibly
by the pure joy to be had
by the two crocs waiting
behind the first

gratuity will not be frowned upon

if
I were
too go belly up
right here
right now,
I'd bet
there
is more
than one who
would suck the marrow
from my bones
but, I gotta say
I wouldn't judge
any one of those
opportunistic jack offs
if I'm there, flat on my
back, the nails of my fingers
dug into my chest, spittle puddling
under my chin, my drawers filled
with excrement
do you honestly
think I am going
to care if there is
a free for all
over the crapola
I spent my money on?
take it,
stab each other
for it,
judge each others
version of social standing,
hire a multitude of
high tone lawyers to
scream at each other in language
you'll pretend to understand

just as long as
you realize
my net
gain
never even
came close
to my
net loss
it just
didn't matter
that goddam much
to me
if anyone thought
I would ever give up
living in pursuit of prestige
they shouldn't
even utter my name,
just keep your
mouth shut,
smile and nod
a little bit at the wake,
and tip
the guy with
the shovel
on your way out

puppet ministry

mid morning down town
open air farmers market
heading back to my
truck with some pinto beans
and a Hubbard squash
I found myself
being evangelicized
by some pine and balsa disciples,
their robes fashioned from scraps
of dish cloths and discarded
dress shirts

badly carved gospel mongers
extolling the promise of salvation
arms waving jerkily
about at the ends of
strings
mouths flapping open
and shut with
irritating little clicks
every time a head cable
was pulled

the puppeteer,
a young woman
of about twenty two or so
would phase her voice through
pitches high and low,
depending on the character,
her face taking on emotions
that the toy prophets could not
she wore too much perfume

it wafted over and around
the cheap folding table that
supported the cardboard and

crêpe paper Jerusalem
it was nearly enough to
burn the eyes
and was heavy with roses
ahhh, roses
the odor of sanctity

knowledge breath

take your time as you
sip my brain through
a silver straw
don't take it all
in a gulp or two
savor it a bit
after it makes it's
way to your
perfect mouth
daintily dab your
glossy lips with
hand stitched linen
and say my name
say it slow and lean in
as you do
I want to smell what
I've learned on your breath

your life

has left an
impression in time -
like a childs
handprint
in plaster
your life
sits on the mantle
of my mind
next to
dried leaves of laurel
among offerings of
icons small and simple
flickering votives
give the years
a familiar
soft glow,
its illuminated
pages open
parchment yellow
brittle
I visit often
a particular year
when your vast
heart beckoned me lay
my head upon the breast
of your world
I stand before
that volume of you
longing to
rest there again,
with one of your hands,
cradling my head
the other spread on my
heaving chest
letting you

pour yourself
into me

string theory

as children we tie a string
to the first thing we love
then we play out the line
as we move along
death may
simply be
the act of
winding the string back
around our hearts and
untying the knot

Gargoyle

a fleshy gargoyle
protruding from
granite library steps
looking west, where the
lake lies, view blocked
by abandoned hotel, a
dragon tail of grey and white
pigeons whips through the
glassy steel maze around me
I can hear the pages in
a book on urban homesteading
whipping back and forth
breeze blows through my hands
my thumb holds the place
where I left off
the obligatory obelisk in
the square points star ward, bronze
warriors look out from within
the circle they form at its base
not a smile among them
I would like to see
a military statue
smile someday
I want to see
a president pick up a rifle
the next time war is declared,
let's see this leader really
lead the young men
and women into battle.
let's see an official declaration actually
signed by God and the country
if it is, as we are told time and again,
in reality, all
for God and country
the tail comes back around
I look away from the cast metal

crowd, their worn patina
shrouded faces
holding grim,
and go back to the pages describing
ways of sustainable living
in this, the age of decline

Bell

it's not the first
ring of a bell
that intrigues me
rather, it is the
diminishing waves
of sound that
pulsate after the
hammer finds its mark
a subsonic aura
that laps over itself
I listen until the timbre,
at its faintest,
finally fades
and becomes
the whisper of
the cosmos
there, spread out
over the experiment
that is humanity
if my consciousness
were to come before
the striker
who would listen
for the modulating
waves rushing outward,
seeking to meld
into the one
perfect tone of
creation

forever blossoms

eight slices of apple
in a paper towel
on his lap
they came from
the tree he planted
the year
his daughter died
one slice for
each year since
with each bite he
came a memory
her small hands
in the dirt
the way she danced
around the newly
planted tree
her asking if she
could have applesauce
for dinner that night
the way she waited by
the window every morning
for weeks to see if any
apples had arrived
waiting forever, she said
for the blossoms

Saved

my mother saved
buttons, buttons
and green stamps
she had enough buttons
to mend every Sunday
shirt that needed mending
from the time she was thirty
on into infinity, and the stamps
she had nearly enough
for that set of curtain rods
she so coveted, right up
until my brother and I
discovered them and found they
stuck to furniture and walls just fine
my father saved
nails, nails
and washers
not so much screws though,
I could never figure that one out
bolts either, plenty of washers
some just the right size
for the gumball machine
up at the Bells IGA market
we never knew or cared what IGA
stood for, but we sure had a cocky
way of walking with our
pockets full of washers and gum
I saved Slurpee cups with
superhero pictures on them
I can't remember now if they
were Marvel or D.C., I'm sure
my friends would remember,
I was always just a fringe player
in the comics game. The cups were
cool though, and served other purposes,

like holding the washers nipped
from my dads' collection
Jesus saves, so the old saw goes.
maybe it's Matchbox cars
or baseball cards, I'm sure
he's got the in on the good ones,
or maybe it's just change
dumped from robe pockets into
pipe tobacco tins at the end of the day
maybe, in times when he's not
busy, he separates out the
wheat back pennies,
and the silver dimes,
I know I would

wooden steps

I sat on the warm wooden
steps contemplating nothing
when a single oak leaf drifted
down and landed on my lap
I looked at the leaf with some
amazement, surely it was an omen
for there wasn't an oak tree
anywhere to be seen
did it signify a pretense to war
or a hope for unity
was it there to confirm that
there is strength one carries
even when separated from
the true source of that strength
as it had carried the strength
of the tree it came from
or was it a symbol for
a love that was about to
descend on me, lightly arousing
me into an awareness of
things that I was dangerously
on the verge of missing
I could only stare at the leaf
try to draw answers from it
after a while I turned it
over, hoping there would be
writing on the other side, I don't
need omens but rather
clear instructions as to
what I'm supposed to do

before the casting out

before the casting
out, there was a
time of lessons

a time when you were still
pliable, when
you could be drawn
in through
eyes of mud chinked stone
and passed out through
labyrinth of tongue
when cast, you flew
until you came upon
a place where
holes
come at you
they fall at you –

on mysterious strings
of vapor, to be
counted as if
on a rosary
they are but the weight
of shadow, yet hold worlds
without measure

they hold worlds with
shorelines of hidden coves
fortressed by stands
of unnamed trees of
unknown origin that
canopy thick between
sky and ground

they hold worlds
thick with grottos

carved into hillsides
dug out for prostrate hermits
who chant
who wail
who stare at bleeding floors
lit by single oil lamp

places full of juggling fools
garbed in colors
of their own imagination
working blind streets
walled by hollow buildings
deaf streets
populated by pigeons
who eat no offerings

lands where mountains
stand sentry before
valleys carpeted with
wheat that stretches
toward the lifeblood
of spring fed streams

a million or more
holes may rain upon you
that first day
they hold within themselves
anything you want
peer into them
pick where you'll fall

Unshattered

I wish that I could
spend an afternoon stuffing
elephants into envelopes
if such a thing were possible
I could take a week
rounding up ants
or an hour or so
counting the branches
of the plum tree in the
neighbors yard
anything would do
anything to get my
mind of off
things like
the scars religion has
left on faith
or how children handle
words such as,
I never knew your father
it would keep me from
listening for hymns on the wind
only to hear cries of battle
it would offer a brief reprise from
the anger a cold hearth brings
or the darkness of a silent doorframe
I would lose for a time the way
I despise the drunk on the corner
as much as the empty bottle
on my nightstand
I would,
if only briefly,
see again
through
unshattered eyes

Here I am

I have hung on the wall
just to the left of the
archway
for years
I came with the place,
eventually relegated to being
another item of
interesting decor
retrieved from a stack
of abandoned things in
a corner of the attic
and used to cover a
light switch that no
longer turns anything on
though you
never knew
who I was,
I became at various
times Aunt Olivia,
Grandma Callister,
the old broad who
used to own the place,
Mary, Queen of Scots
or "not sure,
but we've seen
her ghost"
I've watched as you've
rushed by,
late for some
appointment
and watched your kids sneak
in late at night
I've been an impartial
witness to arguments,
love making,

birthdays
dreaded calls from relatives
twenty one Christmas mornings
twenty one new years' eves
and before that
eighteen years
of the attic ceiling
I had ninety one
years of my own,
seeing
through
the eyes of the living,
saw the world of five cities and
as many children, none of whom
stayed near my final
home, saw the world
of a husband of forty six years
and a neighborhood growing
up around me
I looked out the windows you do
I walked the floors you do
I died in the room you sleep in
I know your names,
though you
not mine,
and I say
a prayer for you
every night

the next day

everything seemed
halflife and yellowedged
duskslung evening
doubtlong meandering wish
she spoke with eyebrow
and fingertiptap,
slow open and close of lids
a slight smile
as I placed my hand on
the arm I knew she
could feel
leaning in to
look into her eyes
wanting to ask
so much about her life
as I ungloved
as I unsmocked
from the door
I was only
able to say softly
I'll come see you
tomorrow or
the next day

grace

one
must
learn grace
when passing
through
a life
because
it is not
a closet that
holds skeletons
but rather
a basket
carried
on the top
of your head

after the reading

after reading what
I wrote, she set the
pages and her glasses
down on the bed beside her
"I like these" she said
she always says that
and asked me
"have you ever written
a poem about me"
"umm..." I said, not much of an
answer I reckon, by the
way she just said "oh"
and picked up the magazine
she was reading when I came in,
looking at me over the
rim of her glasses as
she put them back on
what I really wanted to say was
"I've tried"
but I've never
found a way to properly
describe her
how that even when she
is at her frailest, she is the
only strength I possess
how she fills the valley between
peaks of anger and elation with
a deep lush calm
how she has kept me from
death by stupidity on
innumerable occasions
she has steered our ship away from the
rocks
and has guided our feet on the path
she chronicles our history for following
generations because she knows I'll

forget most or all of it
where I'd have a house, she has built a
home
she knows when I need to sleep
long before I do, she knows when to let
things go.
she is the names
the dates
the times
she keeps the lights on
the fire going
the pantry in order
she can tie a tie
and untie a noose
this is what I wanted
to say for years,
maybe she knows
I think I caught a glimpse
of a smile as I turned
to slink off to the garage
to rearrange things
I just rearranged yesterday

leap

should I trust this guy?
he is standing before
a flaming abyss
a clipboard in one hand
a quill in the other,
a stack of files on the ground
near his sandaled feet
his head looks a bit too
big, almost conical
(not at all what I expected)
o. k. the choices are a bridge
of stone and a bridge of paper...
(man, he smiles a lot, kind of like
a car dealer or a hawker of
nitrous balloons)
is there a third choice?
a tight rope maybe?
I'm used to that
can I try to pole vault across?
if I get up enough steam I bet
I could clear it and make
a stylistically perfect landing
he just grins and motions to
one bridge then the other
c'mon man, seriously?
why isn't the paper one burning?
what's on the other side anyway?
here, let this lady go first
she seems all hopped up to
check out, I'll just hang a while
and see what happens
no? whatever, the paper one then

just like the sound of
the ocean in a shell

I wondered once
when I was a kid,
looking at the head
of an elk mounted
on the wall above my uncles
fireplace
I wondered if I took
it down and put my own head
inside it so I could
look through its eyes
would I be able to see
the forest that he ran in?
the creek he drank from?
his favorite berry patch?
or would I just see my
uncle in his ridiculous Elmer Fudd
flap ear hat and furry top boots?
would I be able to hear my uncles
"ho-holy crap!"
or the elks
"now, what in the hell is that thing?
or the just report of the Winchester
then nothing at all?

scattered

there amassed a
hope-worn population
fearful
recipients of
serrated speculation
    so
      tearfully
        filling voids
in housing mills
shrill laments from
family filled fiberglass
containment
pods, smirking nods
from the cockerel strutting
from holy white bellied
presidential blue winged beast
with the stature of a bar room
non-contender, an eraser with
language of a thief
he rolls his sleeves
he rolls his Connecticut gator eyes
he rolls his tongue up
behind glistening oil bought incisors
revealed in curled lip grin
he who needs the least is
he who holds the solutions reigns
he motions with emblemed
chalice, running it along
the fence bars
fill this up with what
you've left , by the crest
branded on my chest
I swear by Christs
bequest
I will fix

            fix it
it will be fixed
propagandized pain
pontificated plunder
prophesized promise
the low places
awash
the high agleam
the unwanted   away
separated like chaff
afterthoughts
scattered in the tempest that
spun in with thrashing arms
then moved away
offering warning
and her name
for inclusion
in his failed legacy

the morning was

so quiet
I could almost hear
his skull vibrating
every time he drove
his face into
the bark
like a feathered,
loosely tuned snare
and the grub
also, its
tireless burrowing
making
the same scratching
noise
my eyelids do at
2:30 in the morning

breaking the silence

if the silence
becomes a bit
    too
        accurate
we can lend
credibility to the
moment by
losing our senses
and   shaking the walls
we could take on
new
    identities
stomping the jeweled
frocks of decorum
into
horned
masks
of
malice

burdened

I've never been burdened
with being the
apple of someone's eye
which is not a bad thing
staying at that level of performance
is just too damn tiring
I never was the
sharpest knife
or pencil,
or the reddest tomato on the vine
also, I cannot recall
ever being
the tan to anyone's gerine
I have on occasion, however,
been a burr in the side
a thorn in the paw
and a pain in the ass

between shadows

I looked for her over the hedge
that ringed her yard,
on the watch for the deaf,
half blind dog that bit me hard
one time as I turned to call
to her granddaughter
her garden gloves on the rail
of the porch, hat on the rocker
there was a tin pail
of beans on the steps, a crock
of cabbage waiting for salt
but no sign of her
she was known to wander
a little, as happens with
folks her age, walks to ponder
about a life of small gifts,
conversations, plans halted
prayers for grace to occur
one of us would retrieve
her occasionally, helping her
back to her door and would leave
with a smile (we were sure
she would do it all
again) and again we'd return
her home, this time it seems
she had gone for good
off into some complex realm
and we wondered, how long would
that old blind dog, caught
between shadows, wait for her

Joan

a wind advisory came
across the radio, the only
thing on in the room
looking past the woodstove
out the window at the
darkening afternoon
it looked as if a chill
was on the way
so I bunched some paper
under the kindling and struck
the match, as I did
I thought of Joan of Arc
was she listening for
advice on the wind
as the flames grew higher?
or was she content
with the guidance she'd
already
received?
I wondered as I
rubbed my hands
over the stove,
was a door be opened
for her before the flames
got too intense?
lingering was a
thought of flames
meant for me
as I turned to pick up my
gloves and head out
to the woodpile
the axe, after it
made it's way through
the chunk of ash
made a sound just

like that of
a slamming door

Persuasion

like
  lidocained fish hook
    on tendril cast – unfelt
beneath skin it slips
in shifts he is pulled
trying to catch one solid
  grip
the   lodger   tapes
notes to doors
papers
and packages left
  are left
        for other lives
to gather like conclusion
to draw toward raw dot
of satisfaction
to bind within withering blindness
the sight
once gifted

the boy

the boy
was standing where I
wished to be standing
his shirt with the wide
stripes and his cotton
white hair made him
easy to spot in the tall
grasses of the field
he wished not for a
mansion, or even a
one room cabin
as I would have, no
he found happiness in a hollow log
or a fox den for napping
nor did he cry out for
a pot bellied stove and a
fair supply of split wood
to stand by after
an early evening dip, no
he was content drying and
warming himself on the
rocks by the creek
he had a pair of low black
sneakers, but they were laying
at the end of the red dirt trail,
tied together, having been slipped
off the shoulder they were carried on
and forgotten.
I had slick black
shoes on my feet, always
worn but never scuffed, never
forgotten, though I wish I could
forget them and all that brought
them to me.
Them and the white shirt
armor that weighed me down

forget the white shirt and designer
tie and try to dodge
the saber like arms of the clock
that cut deeper with each pass
a horse chestnut hits me in the chest
and falls near my feet
a small laugh comes from
somewhere in the thicket,
a striped apparition darts
behind a pine
"c'mon!" he yells "c'mon!"
I take off my shined shoes
and socks pick up
the sneakers and hang
them over my shoulder, though I knew
they would no longer fit
"c'mon! hurry!"
I took a step off the trail
and could feel the pull
then stepped back,
the tug was alarmingly
familiar
"hey! hey!"
I turned away, fighting
now, resisting the call
his voice started to fade into
the sounds of the field again
as I walked barefoot
away from the vision
back toward my car

body of evidence

a crimson clematis
it's lone blossom
   leading
      the
       vine
      up
   the
    wall
     near
    the
iron gates of the prison
   (like a whisper trying
     to eradicate a shout)
from somewhere unseen
screams rattle teeth
like tin sheets
in hurricane squalls
stung   solo
impresarios
cry   operatic
- tragedy (the incidental music
of political convenience)
men: like oranges peeled
pulsate in
packs the
weakest pushed
to the edge
the rest
lick bitterness
off fingertips
all they feel
is the sweat of the stone
damp with hopelessness
the dirt consuming small
portions of them

their names
(rice paper footnotes)
dropped into
the torrent
of governmental
discharge
undone
in time
interred
unnamed
without a body
of flesh or evidence

be sure to get my good side

I just
turn the bruised
side of the fruit
away from the eyes of
the world. The light, if good,
will show all that's needed
to be seen by
all those also
so damaged.

undeserved

by way of
brutal disregard
I have silenced myself
so it is here
in the vacuum of night
that I sit beside my
my beaten muse,
            trying to
            raise it again
"give me one more chance"
I whisper into its bleeding ears
but it does not move
I brush the matted hair
from loyal eyes
that have now gone grey
its regal head lays
in my lap, lungs
billow no longer
the loving breath
that carried its gifts
to me -
undeserved

blessed

lilac'd eyed sun crowned
you came through
the door with
the dew of dawn
on your shoulders
and I wondered why it
was that you
ever landed here
there is no doubt
that I have been
blessed
as you put
the bouquet in water
and transform into
an aura'd silhouette
at the patio door
eyes of lilac
crown of sun
light of morning
myself
simply
happy

the whole

we move through
this nebulous dimension
cells, always on
the verge but unable to divide
thus is the dichotomy of self
recognition of this
crawls slowly
over the rock falls strewn
between the question
and the answer
slow
the way lines appear
in the face of a man
shedding layers of youth
layers as
thin as
smoke of incense
(almost imperceptible)
it's there in the eyes also
          (in those of humans at least)
the evidence of duality,
the truth that occupies
a brightly lit hall behind
glazed fortress walls
peering through the frosted
glass of learned doubt,
revealing only a backlit silhouette
leaving the mark of a kiss
that will be unseen,
ignored or forgotten
(as gifts often are)
one eye is always a little
different, darker at pupils
edge - eater of light - heavier
here where glaciers carved
the land and left behind

this lake
this lake looked upon by
eyes of a millennia
half saw halos of stars
interlaced
in the walls of ice
that receded, leaving a
vast granite basin filling
with crystalline water
they saw forests rise from mossen
valleys, saw creatures of beauty
and might,
the frail and winged,
the microbial and immense
all take to life here, (and longed
to embrace that life and
fuse themselves into it,
willing to lay bare, a taut muslin
awaiting gesso and pigment)
the other half saw fire
the other half saw ashen
flesh violated by claw and fang
vipers
waiting for those
who by chance dragged themselves
out of black pools onto
scalding shores
the other half saw only
the tattered canvas of a
masterpiece
battered against the rocky
cliffs of eventuality
one hails half the cycle
one the other
neither recognizes
the whole

waiting for the drum

the collective
heart as an
un-taut drum
     lays
        slack
and rings out no
rhythm upon which
we long to be borne
oh, to
hear once more
the sacred phrases
of youth, long
dry on the solemn
and silenced lips
 of all
     who were
        left to watch
their hovels razed
(after being built on
the unsteady pilings of
greed driven compromise)
so say now...
what will spring forth
from a generation whose
tools are warehoused in museums?
what could come
from their era,
as books are left
stacked in shuttered libraries?
what of these? will they be
the ones of songs forgotten?
the ones without compass?
will no one
author a great vision?
or take up
brush and pigment to

create masterpieces derived
from Jeffersonian ideals?
what of these? will they be
the ones to
wear their hands
to dust
knowing that
        there's to be
stone on mud -
mud on stone, 'til
constructed high the partition
takes the form of suspicion
        which
                creates ill
intent and sets apart
the minds of the learned
mournful echoes sweep through
musty halls
where once revered
oracles of
their age held court
what of these? will they be
the ones made to set
mud on stone
stone on mud, 'til
it is so high
that those separated
will only
hear an occasional
question that
happens over by chance
what answers could
be offered from
a generation whose
education hangs upon
its frame as would a lash
scarred hide,
worn raw?

able only to
skim
the surface of
knowledge
Will they be, always
waiting for the drum

The last time I
shot the moon

it shot back
so I don't do
that any more
nor do I sow oats
     (wild or otherwise)
I care not to
go on a tear or a bender
nor am I apt to swing on a star,
no matter how impressively
displayed it's twinkle may
appear to be
     (to the unbiased eye)
thank-you,
but it's enough really
just to peek through the
slats of my blinds
at the people in the
garb of their individual
tribes, avoiding one another
or at the very least,
pointing each
other in the
wrong direction

Winkee the clown contemplates suicide in ol' Missou'

the paint and nose
the oversized shoes
slapping loose
planked boards
and sawdusted dung here
in the mean
center of
the country
with sunflower in hat,
the polka dot pants,
and balloons at
least as twisted as
I've become,
I schlep my way
around the miniature car,
wallowing for the masses
I could have climbed into
the lions cage
or have tormented
the tigers
I could have
badgered the strong man
about his sexual orientation
until he snapped my neck
I could have flown off a trapeze
into the candied cotton crowd
I could have eaten fire,
no... really
any of these would
have done the trick
but I'm quite the
indecisive sort of jester
so as a slide whistle
dirge played
I chose to simply
dig a splinter

of sunshine
out of my eye
with a needle of darkness
leaving myself
unsighted to anything
that may have had a bright
side in this circus

the milkman

most Fridays
when the milkman was done
with his last run of the week
he would come over
and have a few beers
with my father, they would
laugh and gesture as
I moved from one
lap to the other,
listening to their grand tales,
asking a five year olds questions
and offering a five year olds
perspective of the world
to the child version of me
these visits seemed to have
been a natural occurrence,
something to count on as
sure as Bugs on Saturday
after he got the cancer
and died my folks cancelled
the dairy service
my dad kept the box
on the front step
for a year or two
it was a great place to keep
a baseball glove or a dog leash
or any number of small things
that needed to be removed from
the lawn so it could be cut
I came across that old box
in my parents garage one
afternoon a while back,
inside were still a few
things from our childhood
I wondered about the milk man
as I took them out and
looked into the empty

box, felt the dents and the faded
raised paint of the logo of
the dairy that had long since
been closed down
or incorporated into some
milk leviathan
I felt how light
it seemed now
I could still
smell the faint
earthy remains from
it's short stint as a place to
earthy remains from
it's short stint as a place to
raise fishing worms
I wondered how the milkman
made out after his stay in the hall
of departure, was he still
wearing the white shirt with his
name sewn above the pocket?
was he ever aware of his wife's
impending mental instability?
did he have the same
words of kindness and wisdom
for his own boy as he had
for me? where was that boy now?
I made a mental note
as I hugged my dad and
thanked him for onions
he dug up that morning,
it was time to get a box
of my own I thought,
so that, later,
when it is turned in
a future somebody's hands,
it's contents shaken
out on some future garage
floor, I might be one if those
people that is

wondered about
outside of life

another night

another night waiting
       foreign light to
            graze on phantoms
locked in fetal
(the breath some absence
passes through hangs sheer)
"translucent as film on eye..."

snow angel

he sat in snow
by the creek
adolescent boy waiting
for the girl to drift down,
a snowflake come
there to rest
with him,
she was the girl on the sled
with him
she was his now
over the field he brought her
yes, he was her boy...hers
waiting for her to settle
in the creek by the snow

sweepers

they mounted the steeds
of suppression and along
maps plotted with points
of deception,
their veins flowing with
the fear of wide spread
truth, they rode with
swords drawn
slashing birthright and trust,
flying banners of
state security, their
fatted brethren swine
cowering in well banked
fortresses, as patrons
of paranoia
and they,
having chosen this path,
trampled Themis -
after clawing her belly
and biting her breast
          refusing to suckle
they rode on, damp with
fervent exaltation,
rabidly vapid
demanding the same
they came collecting
wires and words
with arms full of stories
to shackle and
snatching frequencies
from the air
severed tongue trophies hang
around their necks
  baricado
    bullhorn
      biblioclasts

who tattoo eyes with
reversed vision and
bust drums of ears with
mallets of malfeasance
actus reus?
"never!"
        they cry
"damnum absque injuria"
        they proclaim
with hands held high
and empty
before it was this way
before I became aware
of the evil
that walks among
the gentle beings
of this place
I could rock a babe
in my arms, her fragile
breaths a steady three
beats per measure
I could float with my twin
on waters serene exchanging
silent comforts and
able to smile
now I am
only hoary and bent
with clouded storms for eyes
that search through
this new history
for anything real

For myself

I promise not to mention
a basket of oranges
or how the curtains
sheer and fluttering
on the soft spoken voice
of an April breeze
are like the wings of
a heavenly messenger
come to my window
to serve me papers of passage
I also
will not drop
a single word
about quiet evenings, the moon
or the rhythmic breath of
the ocean on the golden
shoulders of the shore
In fact,
I have precious little
to say about
warm embraces
fields of clover
or the
eternal light of God
in a childs eye
most times
the thought of
things such as these
on days when
snow piles car-top deep
I prefer to keep
for myself

tick

I have a nervous tick
I picked it up
on a walk in a patch of
woods not far from here
I can't speak too much
to that of which
I'm not certain, but
this tick has seemed
to have lost its
ability
to cope
with dark energy and sin
so I just let it twitch
around behind my left ear
if I don't change
direction too fast, or
play my ear buds too loud,
sometimes it will
come out to check
if the world is still evil
most days
it is and more-
it will then just look around
and nip a little at my neck
then head back up and
settle in, sucking blood
and passing time
a jittery bug I know
but we are all
a bit like the tick
parasitical, wary,
in need of a
kind host

waking up at a mountain retreat one last time

my morning sock
got caught on a nail
that had,
over the years,
worked it's way
up from the floor
just enough, you see,
to do such a thing,
so I was pitched forward
toward the
scenic open window
I thought the
mountain top lake
just beyond the pines
serene, to be sure,
and if not for my fear of
heights and water
a mountain top lake
would be the perfect
place to partake in
activities such as
rowing a boat, or
staking a claim on a blanket
armed with niceties like
finger sandwiches
and chardonnay
this is what I thought
as I fell away from my snared
sock, disobeying balance
the pine scent that
drifted in was sweet
and pungent, lifted by
the dampness a mountain
morning professes
to hold as

it's universal right
and in the few flailing
seconds that remained
it served only to remind me
of the caustic
perfumed cleaner
that got into my nose
and eyes during a janitorial
gig in high school
this was the other
thing that crossed my mind
as I closed the space
between the nail
and the window
and as would be expected,
as I cleared the sill,
and took in
this inverted panorama
a jaybird was
at the ready
with snide
whistling observance
that my style
of flight was
somewhat less
graceful than his
and that I was
heading in entirely
the wrong direction

when I was mud

without form
flow I could
like time
as ash I traveled
further still
when dust was
my being
I found my place
in untouched places
           (for a time)
then
I was water -
finding my own level
carving my own path
now,
as all and none of these,
I can only sit at
the edge of the bed
as memory
slowly unpacks
souvenirs
he is pushing
           flagged pins
           into a map
he is
addressing me by
names I no longer
wear

atom

with each beat
    oftheheart
    ofthecreator
 a universe is born
and
upon the light
thatburst
from
thatheart
I ride
I breathe with every atom
of creation
I sing internal
the original sound
of creation
I am within
the song
of that which
    (within myself)
is the whole of self
I give of
    the whole
        of self
I feel with every atom
all those who are as
the same
those who, with every atom,
sing the
    original
        tone
of all that can't
be known
if only for
the purpose
of knowing
that it is

crosswalk opera

it was her aria
that got me
out of my head
for the briefest of
moments,
rising from under the
diesel drone of the
department of sanitation
truck, taking flight above
the other
city noise
her cane a trident
held high
a plastic dollar store
bag on the wrist
of the fist at her chest
the final note hit
flawlessly

trying to keep up with Chinaski (again)

there is something
about a clean slab
of marble,
leaning nonchalantly
in the darkened
chamber of your days
Italian maybe, quarried by
hands that have long
since worked
their last work
and all that's left
for you is right there
on its polished face
you can stare at
that veined mirror
for hours
waiting for some
life encapsulating phrase
to surface from
the mire of your thoughts
it doesn't blink
it is patient
it's got nothing to
do but mark time,
Hank said it best
I suppose
so, maybe
just maybe
I won't even try

rise the water

rise
  it may
   I know
I'm beginning to float
again,
and rise   rise
the water
rise
  it may
   I know
it has risen
to
this
place now
and oh, so? how is
this time
meant to be?
what
it is
is what vexes
my
days so
tell me dear lady,
will what we hold
as promise be
as a sheaf
left in the field?
tell me, lady, if
I am wrong -
and sing not sorrow
as the port nights grow warm
waste not a summer day
wandering Poes tubercular streets
worrying of
me, for your words
buoy me upon the flood -

my lungs your voice
does fill
with the sweet
breath of life - strife is not
what
I wish to place
on shoulders
that should bear
only the weight
of loving caress
take now
to sleep
and wake to a world
worthy of a woman
such as yourself

Ani Maamin

that cracks in the sidewalk
signify nothing more than
failed structural integrity
nothing by the
small hands of men
will hold up over time
some day, other
hands will steady me
by the wrist and elbow
as I try to navigate
those heaved up sections
my eyes seeing mostly
the past
my heart a sporadically
pulsating balance of
guilt and joy
half way in, I'm lost
but at least I'm looking
at the map now
youthful stubbornness
ebbing
my index finger
tracing the routes drawn
ages ago

accidental aerialist

it was, as the report said
accidental
just a tragic end owed to
curiosity, a need to
experience vistas from
precarious angles
an innocent way
to gain a kinship with
nature...
well... gain kinship he did
flew like a brick he did
feel the wind he did
the sky opened its arms to him
the river bank came to
greet him
the ledge bid him adieu
gravity held up its end of
the bargain
the river glanced up,
quite uninterested
at the accidental aerialist
heading its way

awaiting celestial infusion

I am,
if nothing else,
a product
of the laws of abstraction
you can see what the
prism of life has done
with my element
    dividing
        my light
projecting it on
the pale noon wall
where clear demarcations
can be seen in the hues
each one assigned
to a particular
mood, a certain paranoia
an individual ecstacy
    - the gold at the
        end of this rainbow -
she
walks
in
mornings awash
in amber
she,
alight in her own time
after a rain
when she searches
the sky
for that
ancient arching sign
it is not enough
to let her know
the reason it's not
there, is because

for her,
eternal,
I will keep it
here
on my wall
awaiting
celestial infusion

another sacrificed morning

- it's common fact
boys goof off a bit
        especially
when performing
some menial task
ordered by a loving,
if somewhat
overbearing father
it's also easier to
drift in ones duties
when a fathers motives are
suspect and
when a fathers language is
cryptic and confusing
so how was it, I wonder,
in the awkward silence
that accompanied that trek up
the mountain
did Isaac tried his hand at
juggling?
        sticks of kindling wood
        spinning off into the
        scrub brush
hmmm...
did he,
with deliberate belligerence,
stomp through
puddles of mud
trying to get a little
of the slop onto the robes
of his preoccupied old man?
(who never ceased
waving his hand
in a "get a move on"
motion)

and I wonder if he grumbled
just a little
at this sacrificed morning
looking down
at the place
from where he came
at his cousins
throwing pebbles at sheep
or maybe
at a particular girl
carrying water
back to her families tent

stuck inside of Moav with the
Canaan
blues again

kind of quiet this morning
he thought
sitting on the peak of Nebos
the promised city in sight
rippled by the heat of the desert
it's already crumbling walls
still wondrous to failing eyes
the old guard has died off
the young will carry forth

I put off retirement
for too long anyway
he whispered to the wind
this valley is as good as any
for resting my bones
besides, he had grown tired of arguing
with the boss over every little thing

so there it is, he chuckled
absently stroking
his long dusty beard
the suns sparkles on the river
reminiscent of those that used
to play in his eyes

and there it was,
nearly a half century of service
never called in sick a single day
worked through vacations
never asked for a clothing allowance
always thankful
for the meager fair offered
in the lunchroom

he drew in his last deep breath
and wearily rose, frail hands
around his travel worn staff
he had nothing to do now
but smile, for the first time in quite
a while, and head on down to
his send off party

closet

I don't know how to
speak to the clothes
that hang unworn
on hangers
I could really use
over here on my side
of the closet
or how to address
all of the shoes
pointing their toes accusingly
at me from
their rack
really,
just a nod
of acknowledgment
would be enough
do I ruminate loss
to this drawer of
undergarments
or simply express
thanks for understanding
my ...um,
shortcomings
of the past?
I won't try with
the sweaters
we never got along
and that wide
brimmed Sunday
morning meeting hat
never took kindly
to the way I
stared at it in public
but this scarf here,
we're ok,
it's kinda big

kinda blue
and has penguins
on it
I take it down,
smell it, and put
it around my neck
tonight I'll wear it
at dinner
tonight I'll
wear it to
bed

octotheism

I'm starting to realize
how hard it is to
carry forward with me
this thing called faith
it's heavy and awkward,
a greasy octopus
squirming for escape
or looking to
snatch others away from
their own particular
allegiance
or
it will latch on to mailboxes
or trees or fireplugs
as I make my way along
stopping my progress
so it can flail about
in a show of self promotion
while its oversized eyeball
looks me over,
anticipating my next move
I try to position
its formidable beak outward,
after all, I do haul it around
for protection,
though I admit
not in a very graceful way
I try to avoid the faith
fighting rings that pop
up every now and then,
but I'm weak and occasionally
I'll unwrap the thing and
throw it into the fracas
it's never lost yet
it's never won yet either
just an endless series of

deadlocked matches -
funny how many
trophies are handed out
at these things, considering
afterwards I will pat its bulbous
head and sling it back over
my shoulders
and let it hoist high
it's meaningless
award

Orbs is Buffalo native Fred Whitehead's third collection of poetry. It follows the 2009 release of *Songs, Cradled*, which is made up mostly of his song lyrics from his days in various bands and the 2010 release of *Protected by Paradox*.

This is the second edition of *Orbs*. The first edition was available in 2011 in e-book form only.

Fred currently hosts a poetry reading series in his South Buffalo neighborhood.

Please visit fewhitehead.wordpress.com for more information.

www.ingramcontent.com/pod-product-compliance
Lightning Source LLC
Chambersburg PA
CBHW062020040426
42447CB00010B/2080